CW00328054

THE LIFE & TIMES OF

Oscar Wilde

BY
Timothy Moffet

This edition first published by Parragon Books

Produced by
Magpie Books Ltd
7 Kensington Church Court
London W8 4SP

Illustrations courtesy of: Mary Evans Picture Library;
Christies Images; Bord Fáilte, Dublin; Illustrated London
News

ISBN 1 85813 971 6

A copy of the British Library Cataloguing in Publication
Data is available from the British Library.

Typeset by Hewer Text Composition Services, Edinburgh
Printed in Singapore by Printlink International Co.

OSCAR WILDE

If Shakespeare had been alive and writing at the turn of this century, he might have considered Oscar Wilde as a subject for one of his tragedies of great men brought low.

The progress of this particular great man forms a parabola as cruel and perfect as the stories of Timon of Athens or Coriolanus. As in all the great tragedies, the crux of his life seems to lie at the point where his path takes a sudden downward turn. How is it that such a brilliant, generous and noble man should have become a wretched outcast, pilloried by the same world that once 'licked my conqueror's boots', as he put it in the bitterness of his last days? Does the fault lie with Oscar's own vanity and carelessness, or with a society so immured in hypocrisy that it would happily sacrifice its first-born son merely in order to save face?

Either way, nearly a century after his death, the wit and wisdom of Oscar Wilde still retain their freshness; and his life, a modern morality play, still has powerful lessons for us all.

DUBLIN AND OXFORD

Oscar Wilde was born on 16 October
1854, in an Ireland ravaged by famine
and political discontent. His parents were
middle-class Dubliners who were also re-
markable individuals in their own right.
William Wilde was a distinguished doctor,
a specialist in diseases of the eye. He had a
strong altruistic streak (he was on hand to
give medical treatment to the starving
during the great famine of 1845) and an
interest in Celtic archaeology. His wife Jane
Francesca, niece of the Gothic novelist

Charles Maturin, was a poet and political activist whom William first encountered writing under the name 'Speranza' in the anti-English magazine *The Nation*. Speranza's firebrand oratory dazzled and inspired the young doctor. 'Oh! for a hundred thousand muskets glittering brightly in the light of Heaven, and the monumental barricades stretching across each of our noble streets made desolate by England', she wrote in the issue of 29 July 1848.

Oscar was the second of the Wildes' two sons. Writing to a friend, Jane described her month-old babe as 'large and fine and handsome and healthy . . . He is to be called Oscar Fingall Wilde. Is that not grand, misty and Ossianic?' (She omits to mention his other two names, O'Flahertie and Wills.) To other friends she said she was convinced her second child was destined for 'extraordinary things' but had no such feelings about her first. As the Wildes became rich through William's success – he was appointed Oculist to Queen Victoria and gave consultations to Napoleon III and the Emperor Maximilian – so they moved up in the world. They bought a house in Dublin's elegant Merrion Square, a few doors away from the former residence of the eighteenth-century playwright Sheridan.

The social life of the Wilde household had a chaotic, faintly *louche* flavour, reminiscent in fact of Sheridan's comedies. The house in Merrion Square was perpetually full of guests, who came in droves for concerts, parties and all-night story-telling sessions. Talk was all-important. Speranza's sayings were quoted by all Dublin, as Oscar's *bons mots* would later be picked up by London. The atmosphere was liberal and liberated. The doctor hardly bothered to conceal from Jane his affairs with the divorcees and bohemian women that came to the house, while Speranza carried on a platonic relationship with the astronomer Sir William Hamilton. The little Wildes were always allowed in the company of adult guests – a custom that would have been regarded with horror by genteel English society.

Before long the doctor's sexual appetite and unconventional morals began to get him into trouble, in a way that curiously presages the downfall of his son. One of his former mistresses, Miss Travers, sent anonymous blackmail letters to everyone of any importance in Dublin, describing how she had been drugged and raped by Doctor Wilde. Jane took her baby sons away to the seaside, but the case had already reached the press, and newspaper boys shouted headlines about the 'Frightful Wilde Scandal' in the street outside their boarding-house. The matter eventually came to a close, but the doctor turned to drink, neglected his patients and left his wife and children increasingly to fend for themselves while he retreated to a large country house in County Mayo.

At ten, Oscar was sent to Portora Royal School, then as now Ireland's most prestigious school and a hothouse of classical education *à l'anglaise*. He was a sensitive boy and detested games – 'football is all very well as a game for rough girls, but it is hardly suitable for delicate boys', he said later. Intellectually, however, he shone. His knowledge of Greek and Latin literature astonished his teachers, who had never seen such brilliance in one so young. By the age of twelve he had Virgil and Homer under his belt. In the school holidays he read Keats and Shelley and helped his mother translate Dante and Balzac. If life at home was increasingly miserable – his little sister Isola died at the age of nine, while his father grew both sicker and more blatantly free with his favours to women other than his wife – Portora School was the scene of his first triumphs.

In 1871 Oscar won a scholarship to Trinity College, Dublin, where his intellectual guru and best friend was the Reverend John Pentland Mahaffy, by chance a former guest at Merrion Square. From Mahaffy, Oscar received instruction not only in the refinements of Greek culture – he described him in 1893 as 'my first and best teacher' and 'the scholar who showed me how to love Greek things' – but also in the social arts of hunting, shooting, fishing and witty conversation. Oscar wrote poems and recited them to his fellow undergraduates, who were possibly more interested in drinking and roistering than *belles-lettres*. But he was no shrinking violet: a popular legend has it that when a student laughed at his lily-livered ways he received a knock-out blow from Oscar's right fist.

At Magdalen College, Oxford, where he went at the age of twenty in 1874, Oscar was happier than at any other time – it was, in his words, 'the most flower-like time' in his life. 'In Oxford, as in Athens, the realities of sordid life were kept at a distance', he wrote to his friend Frank Harris, '. . . everywhere the aristocratic feeling: one must have money, but must not bother about it. And all the appurtenances of life were perfect; the food, the wine, the cigarettes; the common needs of life became artistic symbols, our clothes even won meaning and significance.' He cast off his old-fashioned Dublin suits, and his checked tweed jackets, cravats and wide-brimmed hats were the talk of the town. As at Trinity, his aesthetic whims occasionally produced the wrong reaction, but he knew how best to deal with any problems. On one occasion, a gang of hearties was about to pulverize Oscar's collection of blue and white china (made newly fashionable by the Pre-Raphaelites). Oscar seized the leader of the gang and smashed him almost to smithereens, after which he said with relish, 'And now, give me the pleasure of tasting a bottle of excellent brandy.'

He wrote poetry, kept a commonplacebook which he filled with clever epigrams, went boating on the river, and spent more money than he possessed on entertaining friends in his rooms, which looked out through a Gothic window over the river. He swam in all the intellectual currents of the time, meeting both John Ruskin and Walter Pater, and absorbing their diverse influences in the realm of aesthetic theory. In terms of religion, he wrote that he was 'swaying between Romanism (Manningism) and

Atheism'. His circle of friends were well-born fellow-worshippers of Beauty, languid youths like Reginald Harding ('Kitten'), William Ward ('Bouncer', for a time Oscar's favourite), and Hunter Blair ('Dunsky'). Oscar's nickname was 'Hosky'. None of them had a clear idea what he wanted to be, but Oscar had a notion that, 'Somehow or other, I'll be famous, and if not famous, notorious'.

His time at Oxford was a mixture of blazing success (he won the Newdigate Prize for his poem 'Ravenna') and failure treated with an impudence that outraged the authorities. He hated theology, and, arriving late for an examination in that subject, he was told to copy out Chapter 27 of the Acts of the Apostles as a punishment – or so the story goes. After a while he was told he could stop copying, but half an hour later the examiners noticed he was still writing. 'I was so inter-

Oscar Wilde in his prime

The Wilde family home in Dublin

ested I couldn't leave off', he explained. 'It
was all about a man named Paul who went
on a voyage, and I was afraid he would be
drowned. But do you know, he was saved;
and when I found out he was saved I thought
of coming to tell you.'

LONDON

Almost as influential as Oxford were Oscar's travels in Italy and Greece, made in the spring of 1877, before his final year. He was short of money, as always, but his friends Dunsky and Bouncer were already in Rome and his former tutor Mahaffy was on his way to Greece. The plan was to travel with the latter as far as Genoa and meet up with the former. In Italy, Oscar and his friends saw Ravenna (hence the poem), Venice and Genoa, where Guido Reni's Saint Sebastian struck him as 'the most beautiful picture I ever saw'.

But nothing in Italy made such an impression on the young poet as did the wonders of Greece. Copies of Swinburne and Keats under his arm, he marvelled at Corfu, Zante, Mycenae, the Acropolis and the ruins of Olympia. An excavation was underway at Olympia, and Oscar later claimed to have seen 'the great Apollo . . . raised from the swollen river. I saw his white outstretched arm appear above the waters.' Oscar sighed after shepherd-boys and wrote reams of ecstatic, rather bad poetry. Glutted with beauty, he was late back to Oxford that autumn and punished with a fine of half his bursary – 'for being the first Oxonian to visit Olympia', as he ruefully put it.

Meanwhile Oscar's father had died, bequeathing mostly debts to his wife and offspring. Jane, her income drastically reduced, decided to sell the house in Merrion Square and move to London. Oscar, now almost penniless, feared he would have to do 'some horrid work to earn bread. The world is too much for me. However, I have seen Greece and had some golden days of youth.' In late 1879 he made his way to London (his mother and brother Willie were to settle there permanently the following year) and found rooms in Salisbury Street, off the Strand, which he shared with the painter Frank Miles.

Oscar wasted no time in charming his way into the highest echelons of London society. A friend he had made at Oxford, Lord Ronald, whose family owned huge swathes of Scotland and a clutch of immense country houses, proved the perfect passport to a glittering new world. Ronald knew Sarah Bernhardt from Paris; he was a friend of such diverse personages as Ruskin, Carlyle and the Empress Eugénie. His sister ruled the ballroom at Grosvenor House with its Gainsboroughs and Rubens, where Oscar became a regular fixture.

Drawing-rooms all over London vied with each other to receive a visit from this extraordinary young man, who dressed in green velvet and silk stockings and bewitched the ladies with his amusing stories. Just over a year after his arrival he was summoned by the Prince of Wales, who coined the somewhat Wildean maxim 'I do not know Mr Wilde, and not to know Mr Wilde is not to be known'. In no time at all Oscar became the unofficial jester at a court of princes, painters, heirs and famous actresses like Ellen Terry, who inspired Oscar's first sally into theatre, the melodrama *Vera: or, the Nihilists*. He insinuated himself into the fashionable intelligentsia known as the 'Souls', and dazzled them above all with the brilliance of his repartee, set-piece stories and meditations, which had more in common with oratory than conversation. His outrageous wit often appeared to poke fun at conventional Victorian attitudes. 'To get into Society these days one has either to feed people or shock people – that is all', he said. He affected laziness, moral decadence and effeminacy, and his audience begged for more.

In 1881 Oscar reprinted his poem 'The New Helen', written two years before, with a new dedication: 'To Helen, formerly of Troy, now of London'. This referred, as all of London knew, to Mrs Lillie Langtry, the twenty-year-old actress and heroine of any aesthete worth his salt. Within a few months of her arrival in London from Jersey, Lillie had been painted by Millais, Burne-Jones and Whistler and immortalized in marble by Frederick Leighton. Like the rest of the city's young men, Oscar fell divinely in love with her, but his infatuation went further than most. It was known that he had asked for the entire contents of a flower-shop to be sent to Mrs Langtry's home at 18 Pont Street. What Mr Langtry thought of such an extravagant amorous gesture is not known. But soon Oscar and 'the Lily' became firm friends, and could be seen parading the streets in matching costume.

When not courting actresses or entertaining aristocrats, Oscar found time to pay his mother a visit at her Sunday salon in Chelsea. Jane moved in less rarefied social circles than he, but the arrival of her son with one of his 'Professional Beauties' never failed to shed glamour on her own proceedings.

Mother and son could never bear to be too far apart. In 1880 he and Frank Miles moved to a small house in Tite Street, Chelsea, which was to be the stage for some of the most dramatic and glorious scenes of Oscar's life. Chelsea was then the fashionable hub of artistic London, home to James Whistler, Dante Gabriel Rossetti and the lesbian novelist Violet Paget, alias Vernon Lee. The Pre-Raphaelite movement, with its headquarters in Cheyne Walk, was in full flower, and pale women could be seen tripping down the King's Road in togas. Ruskin's aesthetic theories were on the tip of every tongue. It all amounted to a Cult of Beauty of which Oscar was rapidly becoming one of the High Priests. Transfiguration came with the parody of Oscar as the Swinburnean poet Bunthorne in Gilbert and Sullivan's *Patience*. Bunthorne is imagined 'walking down Piccadilly with a poppy or a lily in his medieval hand' and suggesting that the uniform of the Dragoon Guards be redesigned 'in spider-web grey velvet which, trimmed with Venetian leather and Spanish lace, topped with something Japanese, would at least have the look of old Eng-

A society ball

Lillie Langtry

land'. But the satire was affectionate, and Oscar lapped it up. In fact he had never walked down Piccadilly with a flower in his hand, but the nation now believed he had. As he put it, 'To have done it was nothing, but to make people believe one had done it was a triumph.'

Fame, or rather notoriety, was all very well, but he had achieved it on the slenderest basis. There was only one play, no prose of any substance, no fiction and a scattering of short poems. When *Poems* came out in the summer of 1881, it sold well but was poorly reviewed – and with some justification, for the writing is a barely-disguised patchwork of imagery culled from Pater, Verlaine and Keats. *Punch* summed it up cruelly as 'Swinburne and water'. Most woundingly, the copy requested by the Oxford Union library was returned to the author on the basis that the poems it contained were 'for the most part not by their putative father at all, but by a number of better-known and more deservedly reputed authors'. On the other hand, both Matthew Arnold and John Addington Symonds were sent a copy and wrote back modestly appreciative letters. 'England is enriched with a new poet', wrote Oscar Browning in the *Academy*.

But perhaps the most serious consequence of the book had to do with Oscar's living arrangements. Canon Miles, father of Oscar's house-mate, complained of the moral indecency of a work like 'Charmides' with its vision of copulation with a statue. The Canon suggested it was time his son end his association with this degenerate poet. 'If in sadness I advise a separation for a time', he wrote, 'it is . . . because you do not see the risk we see in a published poem that makes all who read it say to themselves, "this is outside the province of poetry", "it is licentious and may do great harm to any soul that reads it".' As it happened Frank had almost been the subject of a scandal involving a thirteen-year-old girl, but of this the good Canon was naturally unaware. Meanwhile Frank upheld his father's line, and there was no choice for Oscar but to move out. It was not the last time he would fall victim to hypocrisy.

MARRIAGE

Oscar now needed a new direction and a new source of income. In the autumn of 1882 it seemed he had found both, when the impresario Richard D'Oyly Carte suggested a lecture-tour of America. *Patience* was playing to packed houses on Broadway, but the public had never seen a real live aesthete in the flesh. This would be their chance. Oscar would dress in his usual finery, recite a poem or two and discourse a little on the subject of The Beautiful, and the United States would fall at his feet just as London had done.

Things did not go exactly as planned. The trip started off well, with a few widely-publicized witticisms at the harbour ('I was disappointed in the Atlantic' and 'I have nothing to declare except my genius'). He was instantly swept up in the social mêlée. As he told Norman Forbes-Robertson, 'I am torn to bits by Society. Immense receptions, wonderful dinners, crowds wait for my carriage . . . girls very lovely, men simple and intellectual . . . I give sittings to artists, and generally behave as I have always behaved – *dreadfully*.' He met everyone of importance, from General Grant to the Vanderbilts, from Harriet Beecher Stowe to Walt Whitman ('What a fine boy', said Walt). However, his gospel of Beauty often fell on deaf ears, particularly in such unpromising terrain as Denver and Salt Lake City, where he must have seemed like a being from another world. It was remembered for many years after in San Francisco that his conversational opening had been 'Do you yearn?' But embarrassment or amusement were only the mildest forms of American objection to his aesthetic creed. In Rochester, New York, he was practically booed off the stage. By the end of the tour Oscar was having to fend off hostile journalists, some of whom turned up at the port to jeer at this effete Irishman. As he stepped on board he took his leave of America with another perfectly timed aphorism, but it was poison-tipped: 'For you, Art has no marvel, Beauty no meaning, and the Past no message.'

The following year, bored once more with the salons of Chelsea and Mayfair, he went on another aesthetic jaunt, to Paris, where he finished another mediocre play, *The Duchess of Padua*, and the Baudelairean long poem 'The Sphinx'. In May 1884 he was married to Constance Lloyd, daughter of a Dublin barrister.

Figures on a beach, by James Whistler

Oscar lectures in New York

There can be no doubt that, if not actually a calculated ploy, Oscar's marriage certainly took place at an opportune moment. Both in Paris and London there had been whisperings about his sexuality (*Punch* had called him a 'Mary-Ann') which would now be silenced. There was also the question of money, always a major theme in his life. Constance Lloyd was not rich, but she had at least a regular income from her father and would be worth £1000 a year when her grandfather died.

Though it must have seemed like a good idea at the time, in fact the marriage was to prove one of Oscar's gravest mistakes. For the moment, however, the couple were adoringly in love. She was a quiet, principled, rather serious girl, whose lack of a sense of humour was doubtless outweighed by her mesmerizing pre-Raphaelite beauty. She was, Oscar wrote to a friend, 'very grave and mystical . . . quite perfect except that she does not think Jimmy (Whistler) the only painter that ever really existed . . .: however, she knows I am the greatest poet, so in literature she is all right.' It was clear that on certain subjects Constance had her own opinions. Signs of strain can surely be detected in the following remark of hers, made in the course of one of the couple's endless discursive letters: '. . . I am afraid that you and I disagree in our opinion on art for I hold that there is no perfect art without perfect morality, whilst you say they are distinct and separable things.'

They were married in May and, after a honeymoon in Paris, moved back into 16 Tite Street, which had been fashionably redecorated, mostly in white. Oscar threw himself briefly into interior design and the notion of Good Taste, which he thought could be imparted to the ignorant. While still in the mood for domesticity he was offered the editorship of *Woman's World*, a task he performed for two years with ever-decreasing enthusiasm until he was sacked. The magazine was apparently becoming too literary – with features as serious and highbrow as Sarah Bernhardt on 'The History of my Tea-Gown', it is hard to believe.

Constance bore Oscar two sons, Cyril and Vyvyan, in quick succession. The Wildes looked like a happy family, but there were already cracks in the façade. Oscar was becoming bored with his wife's conventional attitudes, and she had had enough of pose and glamour. A revealing anecdote is recounted by Robert Ross, one of Oscar's most faithful (or least faithless) friends and his eventual literary executor. 'Oscar talked during lunch as I had never heard him talk before – divinely . . . Humour, tale, epigram, flowed from his lips and his listeners sat spell-bound under the influence. Suddenly in the midst of one of his most entrancing stories – his audiences with wide eyes and parted mouths, their food untasted – his wife broke in: "Oh, Oscar, *did* you remember to call for Cyril's boots?" ' Before long it was necessary to conceal his country-house weekends, his outings with actresses, with a veil of duplicity. Constance firmly believed he had taken up golf and played it for two or three hours a day. 'The one charm of marriage is that it makes a life of deception absolutely necessary for both parties', said Oscar; but in this case the deception was one-sided.

SUCCESS AND BOSIE

Until now, the master of the witty aside and
the needle-sharp rejoinder had not managed
to commit to paper anything of more than
passable literary merit. 1888 saw the first real
flowering of his genius, with the publication
of *The Happy Prince and Other Tales*, a
collection of aesthetic fairy-stories. Many of
these were originally written for Oscar's rich
female friends (Princess Alice of Monaco,
Margot Tennant, and Lady Desborough)
but are now assured of their place in the
canon of classic children's literature. *The*

Happy Prince, the bittersweet story of a statue in love with a swallow (shades of the sculptural passion in the early poem 'Charmides'), was apparently the product of an evening spent in the company of some young men at Cambridge University. One of these young men was Harry Marillier, first in the long line of bright young things whom Oscar was to befriend, briefly adore and finally cast aside in favour of another. At first there seems not to have been a sexual element: it is all rapturous lyricism, with only the merest undercurrent of suggestiveness. He writes to Harry, 'You too have the love of things impossible – *l'amour de l'impossible* (how do men name it?) . . . There is an unknown land full of strange flowers and subtle perfumes, a land of which it is joy of all joys to dream, a land where all things are perfect and poisonous.'

Next of the young things was Robert Ross, sent down from Cambridge for criticising the Dean in a university magazine. Ross was an avid fan of all things Aesthetic, from the long hair to the affectations of immorality. According to Ellmann's biography, it was Ross who probably introduced Oscar Wilde to homosexuality, even though he was only seventeen at their first meeting in 1886. It is Ross, believes Ellmann, who is enshrined in *The Portrait of Mr W H*, a brilliant literary detective-story in which the 'onlie begetter' of Shakespeare's sonnets is found to be the fascinating boy-actor Willie Hughes; indeed Oscar told Ross, 'the story is half yours, and but for you it would not have been written.'

As Oscar began to lose interest in his wife, so he began to surround himself with young men; the poets John Gray, Richard Le Gallienne and Andre Raffalovich, his future biographer Robert Sherard, the future art historian Bernard Berenson, Robbie Ross and, eventually, Lord Alfred Douglas, whom he first met at Tite Street in 1891. Something of the flavour of Oscar's relationships with his 'dear boys' can be gleaned from a letter to Le Gallienne in 1890, in which he praises the latter's work and then writes, 'I hope the laurels are not too thick across your brow for me to kiss your eyelids'. In the same year as this letter, Oscar may or may not have contributed to a homo-erotic novel called *Teleny*, published in a secret edition by the bookseller Charles Hirsch, who regularly supplied Oscar with titles like *Sins of the Cities of the Plain*. Little by little, he was discovering the underworld, and relishing the thrill of danger it gave him.

On the surface of things, Oscar was busier than ever. He had abandoned the shallow theatricality of his foppish 1880s persona and was busily formulating a new creed of artifice over nature ('Art for Art's Sake') and wickedness over moral rectitude. The two dialogues, *Pen, Pencil and Poison* and *The Decay of Lying*, can be said to deal broadly with the same theme: the paradox that art creates life. As well as being a theory of artistic creation it was also a kind of vindication of Oscar's new way of life: the implication is that lying, pretence and duplicity are all worthier ways of being than honesty, sincerity and 'truth'. 'The first duty in life is to assume a pose', said Oscar. 'What the second duty is, no one yet has found out.'

The spectacular product of his theorizing, and the work which more than any other sums up the final decade of the nineteenth century in England, was Oscar's only real novel, *The Picture of Dorian Gray*.

The story of a man who remains eternally young while his portrait decays was inspired by the painter Basil Ward ('Basil Hallward' in the novel), whom Oscar had once watched painting a handsome young man. Ward had remarked of his sitter, 'How delightful it would be if he could remain exactly as he is, while the portrait aged and withered in his stead.' *Dorian Gray* was not completely original – there are too many traces of Poe, Balzac, Robert Louis Stevenson and French Symbolism for that – but literary London had never seen anything like it. The book whipped up a controversy when it was published in June 1890 in Lippincott's *Monthly Magazine*. Critics objected to what they saw as its tedium and immorality, and complained that the book was a blatant piece of self-publicity. Oscar responded to the latter charge with typically Wildean languor: 'I wrote this book entirely for my own pleasure. Whether it becomes popular or not is a matter of absolute indifference to me.' The charge of immorality was harder to answer, despite his claim that the book was in fact 'too moral'. 'The story – which deals

Constance Wilde

Fashionable theatre-goers in a box

with matters only fitted for the Criminal Investigation Department of a hearing in camera – is discreditable alike to author and editor', thundered the *Scots Observer*, whose invocation of the law sends a chill down the spine. 'Mr Wilde has brains, art, and style; but if he can write for none but outlawed noblemen and perverted telegraph-boys, the sooner he takes to tailoring (or some other decent trade) the better for his own reputation and the public morals.' (The reference to noblemen was presumably meant to remind readers of the recent scandal involving Lord Arthur Somerset and a group of telegraph-boys in a male brothel in Cleveland Street. Lord Somerset had been forced into exile under a cloud of shame. Oscar may have recognized the omens, but clearly chose to ignore them.)

Oscar's mother wrote from her headquarters in Chelsea, 'It is the most wonderful piece of writing in all the fiction of the day . . . I nearly fainted at the last scene.' Perhaps the most valuable compliment of all came from the great French poet Mallarmé, who confessed that the book's 'deep fantasy and very strange atmosphere took me by storm. To make it so poignant and human with such astonishing intellectual refinement, and at the same time to keep the perverse beauty, is a miracle that you have worked through the use of all the arts of the writer.'

For the next half-decade – the last five years before his downfall – two things were notable in Oscar's life. One was the string of successful plays that poured from his pen: *Lady Windermere's Fan* in 1892, *A Woman of No Importance* and *Salomé* in 1893, *An Ideal Husband* and *The Importance of Being Earnest* in 1895. There was nothing in his earlier stage works to foreshadow either the sparkling frivolity of *Earnest* or the overripe orientalism of *Salomé*. But Oscar was a genius at marketing. He understood that 1890s London had had enough of over-stuffed melodramas and wanted something new. In *Lady Windermere* and the comedies, he gave them something witty, trivial and perfectly constructed. In *Salomé*, which was written in French for Sarah Bernhardt but never performed in London thanks to the Lord Chamberlain's ruling that biblical characters could not be shown on stage, he gave them sublime decadence in the ultra-fashionable French manner.

The second, and in some ways more important, aspect of these years was the arrival on the scene of Lord Alfred Douglas, known by his family, friends and lovers as 'Bosie'. He and Oscar met in 1891, and a year later Oscar was dedicating a copy of his *Poems* 'To the Gilt-Mailed/Boy/at Oxford/in the heart/of June'. It was very soon obvious that Bosie was the love of Oscar's life. This was a passion he pursued with wild extravagance and an almost total disregard for caution.

It was unfortunate that this beautiful and intelligent young man should have a father as aggressive and irascible as John Sholto Douglas, 8th Marquess of Queensberry. The Marquess was a mess of contradictions: best known for establishing the Queensberry Rules of boxing, he was also a writer of poetry (some of which his son published in the Oxford magazine 'The Spirit Lamp'), a hater of Christianity who once interrupted a performance of Tennyson's *The May Queen* to rage against the play's treatment of atheism, and a notorious womanizer who habitually brought his mistress to stay with his wife.

Oscar and Bosie were a couple. Most of London knew this, and those who didn't

Illustration for *Salomé*, by Aubrey Beardsley

The Theatre Royal, Haymarket

know must have suspected it. Oscar showered his lover with money and gifts which he could ill afford. They walked in to dinner through the front door of the Cafe Royal: Bosie, who had his father's fierce temper, would say 'I won't have you come in by the side door. I won't tolerate it. I insist on your coming in by the main entrance with me; I want everyone to say "There goes Oscar Wilde and his minion".' They wrote letters to each other in which high-flown language barely concealed a powerful charge of eroticism. These letters frequently found their way into the hands of blackmailers, and Oscar would have to pay them off with £25, £60 or more, depending on the contents of the letter and, as Oscar liked to joke, on its literary merit. Bosie lent a coat to one of his rent-boy friends, Alfred Wood, leaving in its pockets several letters from his lover. Wood successfully blackmailed Oscar at the theatre where *A Woman of No Im-*

portance was in rehearsal, but decided to keep one of the letters. One by one the pieces of Oscar's destiny were falling into place: this was the damning 'Hyacinth' letter, read out by the prosecution at his trial. It was written from Babbacombe, a country house in Devon which Oscar rented in early 1893. 'My Own Boy,' it read, 'Your sonnet is quite lovely, and it is a marvel that those red rose-leaf lips of yours should have been made no less for music of song than for madness of kisses. Your slim gilt soul walks between passion and poetry.'

One of the saddest aspects of Oscar's drama is the part played by his family. Oscar excluded them from his life with an efficiency that was almost ruthless. He acquired the habit of staying in hotels, so that he could bring boys back after taking them to dinner. On one occasion his wife Constance came to his room in the Savoy bearing his post and begging him to come home. Pierre Louÿs was in the room at the time and heard Oscar say, 'I've made three marriages in my life, one with a woman and two with men!' He occasionally visited his children and told them some magical bedtime story, but cruelly pretended to his friends not to care for them.

Meanwhile he consorted with rent-boys who exploited him for all the champagne and cigarette-cases he could lavish on them. He took Sidney Mavor (later to become a priest in the Church of England) to Paris for the publication of *Salomé* in February 1893. He often took Bosie to a male brothel in Westminster, where Oscar would hold court in the sitting-room among the cockney boys, many of whom were doubtless dreaming up their next blackmail attempt.

Bosie was neglecting his studies at Magdalen and this, together with the public nature of

his homosexual affair, enraged his father the
Marquess, who began to send him furious
letters. Bosie responded to these with venom
and insults. The lovers too began to quarrel.
Oscar had agreed to allow Bosie to translate
Salomé from French into English for an
edition to be illustrated by Aubrey Beardsley. His work, however, was inaccurate and
unacceptable, and Oscar told him so. Bosie
flew into a tantrum, Oscar stood firm, and
for a while it seemed the relationship might
break up. Perhaps Oscar might have saved
himself from total ruin if it had.

With hindsight, there were so many bad
omens in these nerve-racking years that
one would have had to be blind, optimistic
or masochistic not to take heed of them.
Oscar was somehow all of these things at the
same time. In late 1893 both he and Bosie
were caught up in a mysterious scandal,
hushed up before it became public knowl-

edge, involving a sixteen-year-old school-
boy inveigled into sleeping with them at
Oscar's house in Goring-on-Thames and
sent back to school three days late. The
boy's father, an army officer, decided not
to prosecute.

At dinner after the opening night of *A
Woman of No Importance*, the society palmist
Cheiro read Oscar's hands. The left hand, he
said, suggested a brilliant success; the right,
an impending disaster. 'The left hand is the
hand of a king, but the right is that of a king
who will send himself into exile.' Oscar
wanted to know when this would happen.
'At about your fortieth year', said Cheiro –
in other words, within two years.

But Oscar thrived under pressure, and these
two years were creatively among the most
fruitful of his life. While Bosie was away in
Egypt, affording them both a much-needed

break in their increasingly combustible relationship, he finished the last three acts of *An Ideal Husband* and also wrote the short plays *A Florentine Tragedy* and *La Sainte Courtisane*. In the summer of 1894 he began his most famous and greatest work, *The Importance of Being Earnest, A Trivial Comedy for Serious People*. It is brilliantly constructed and dramatically perfect. It dazzles with the wit, warm-heartedness and intelligence of an artist at the height of his powers.

The Importance of Being Earnest

Cartoon of Wilde in *Vanity Fair*

ARREST AND IMPRISONMENT

On 1 April 1894 the Marquess of Queensberry saw his son lunching with Oscar Wilde at the Café Royal. That evening he wrote to Bosie to denounce 'the most loathsome and disgusting relationship as expressed by your manner and expression . . . No wonder people are talking as they are.' Bosie fired back a telegram: 'WHAT A FUNNY LITTLE MAN YOU ARE.' It was not exactly a clever piece of diplomacy, and his father's next letter laid his cards on the table in no uncertain terms: 'If I catch you again with that man I will make a public scandal in a way you little dream of; it is already a suppressed one.' Queensberry began to threaten his son's lover to his face. Oscar later wrote in *De Profundis* that he had gone 'from restaurant to restaurant looking for me, in order to insult me before the whole world, and in such a manner that if I retaliated I would be ruined, and if I did not retaliate I would be ruined also'. But Bosie continued to taunt his father, aware perhaps that he had nothing to lose except his allowance, and he could no doubt make up for that out of Oscar's pocket.

The storm seemed to have died down by the start of 1895, when the two of them went to Algeria with André Gide. Gide was told about Queensberry's threats, and warned: 'But if you go back, what will happen? Do you realise the risk?'. 'That, one can never know,' replied Oscar. 'My friends advise me to be prudent. Prudent! How could I be that? It would mean going backward. I must go as far as possible. I cannot go any further. Something must happen . . . something else . . .' On 14 February *The Importance of Being Earnest* opened to wild acclaim, and two weeks later the 'something else' he'd been looking for began to happen. Dropping in at the Albemarle Club, Oscar was handed a card by the porter: 'To Oscar Wilde, posing as a somdomite'(sic). It was the last straw. Chivvied on by Bosie, who had installed himself at the Avondale Hotel and was running up enormous bills, Oscar decided to sue Queensberry for libel and end the war between them in one final battle.

It was a battle he was sure to lose, as some of his closest friends tried to convince him. Queensberry had engaged the lawyer Sir

George Lewis, ironically an old family-friend of the Wildes, and amassed a large body of evidence which included a list of the boys he was supposed to have had 'indecent relations' with. In spite of his success with *Earnest*, public opinion was now against him.

But perhaps the greatest misfortune of all was to be faced in court by a barrister as brilliant and cunning as Sir Edward Carson. At the trial on 3 April 1895, Carson's cross-examination opened with questions about the moral unhealthiness of such works as *The Picture of Dorian Gray*. Oscar having fended off that charge, saying that the novel could only be seen as perverted by 'brutes and illiterates', Carson turned to the testimony of Charley Parker, Sidney Mavor, Fred Atkins, and Oscar's other rent-boy contacts. Finally the name of Walter Grainger came up, and this was the moment where Oscar made his fatal mistake. 'Did you ever kiss him?' asked Carson, slyly. 'Oh, dear no. He was a peculiarly plain boy. He was, unfortunately, extremely ugly.' Carson moved in for the kill. 'Was that the reason you did not kiss him?' Oscar was rattled: 'Oh, Mr Carson, you are impertinent and insolent . . . You sting me and insult me and try to unnerve me; and at times one says things flippantly when one ought to speak more seriously. I admit it.' His case was as good as lost. A few minutes later it was utterly lost: the judge ruled that the Marquess of Queensberry had been justified in calling Wilde a sodomite in the public interest.

After this catastrophe it was obvious to everyone that Oscar would be arrested. He had a few hours in which to flee the country – the delay is still thought by some to have been an official act of mercy – and indeed he half thought of catching the boat-train from

Victoria, but instead sat drinking hock and seltzer in the Cadogan Hotel. He seemed listless and tired. 'The train is gone. It is late,' he said. At just after six o'clock Oscar was arrested by two detectives.

Oscar may not have made it to France, but dozens of handsome young men, decadent artists, and others who felt it might not do to be around for his trial, certainly did. Both *An Ideal Husband* and *The Importance of Being Earnest* closed in mid-run. Society, in league with the Press whom Oscar had often reviled, closed ranks. Jerome K Jerome, whose *Three Men in a Boat* Oscar had admired, demanded 'the heads of the five hundred noblemen and men-of-the-world who share his turpitude and corrupt youth'. Few of his friends stuck by him. Some of the most loyal were Ada Leverson (known as 'The Sphinx'), who campaigned for Oscar in political circles; Robbie Ross, who was a

Oscar Wilde with Lord Alfred Douglas

Portrait of Wilde by Aubrey Beardsley

constant help to Oscar before, during and
after the trial; and Percy Douglas, Bosie's
brother, and the Reverend Stewart Head-
lam, who together put up bail of £5500,
though the latter barely knew the defendant.

With or without the final verdict, Oscar's life
was already in ruins. He was declared bank-
rupt at the end of April and his most precious
possessions – including Carlyle's writing-
desk, drawings by Burne-Jones and Whistler, manuscripts and first editions – were
sold by auction at Tite Street. Constance
Wilde, stunned by grief, had taken her
children to the country, as Oscar's mother
had done during the Mary Travers scandal of
1864.

The trial was a dismal affair whose conclu-
sions, given the moral climate of the time,
were more or less a *fait accompli*. During a
three-week break between sessions, Oscar

was hounded from hotel to hotel by Queensberry and his thugs, and ended up collapsing on the doorstep of his brother Willie's house, crying, 'Willie, give me shelter or I shall die in the streets'. Once again there was a chance of escape, and even Percy Douglas, who could barely afford to lose his contribution to the bail money, begged that 'if there is a chance, even, of conviction, for God's sake let him go'. But Oscar would not go. As he wrote to Bosie just before the final trial, 'I decided that it was nobler and more beautiful to stay . . . I did not want to be called a coward or a deserter. A false name, a disguise, a hunted life, all that is not for me.' Perhaps he was right, and so was W B Yeats when he wrote, 'I have never doubted, even for an instant, that he made the right decision, and that he owes to that decision half of his renown.'

On the Queen's Birthday, 25 May, the Solicitor-General Sir Frank Lockwood finally turned to the man in the dock and described this as 'the worst case I have ever tried . . . That you, Wilde, have been the centre of a circle of extensive corruption of the most hideous kind among young men, it is . . .impossible to doubt. I shall, under such circumstances, be expected to pass the severest sentence that the law allows. In my judgement it is totally inadequate for such a case as this. The sentence of the Court is that . . . you be imprisoned and kept to hard labour for two years.'

THE FINAL YEARS

And so began the sad final act of the life of Oscar Wilde. The scenes were first Pentonville and Wandsworth prisons, where he slept on a hard bed, dined on weak gruel, suet and water, and suffered appallingly from disease and psychological strain. His suffering was compounded by Bosie's publication of their love-letters, against the advice of Oscar's friends and family and the wishes of Oscar himself. He was then transferred to Reading Prison, having had to wait for half an hour at Clapham Junction station in front

Paris in the 1890s

Oscar Wilde towards the end of his life

of a jeering crowd. Constance (now Constance Holland – she had changed her name) visited him on 19 February 1896, writing afterwards, 'they say he is quite well, but he is an absolute wreck compared to what he was'. (She would die two years later, effectively removing Oscar's last source of income, since she had agreed to pay him a small allowance.) He was able to read widely and write letters, notably the long, bitter and powerfully moving 'Encyclical Letter', to Lord Alfred Douglas, known as *De Profundis*.

As soon as he was released he made for France under the guise of Sebastian Melmoth – a double allusion to the tortured martyr and to the Wanderer of his great-uncle Charles Maturin's novel. He had little money, and settled eventually in the Normandy village of Berneval, moving finally to Paris for the publication of his last important piece of writing, *The Ballad of Reading Gaol*.

The Melmoth persona worked for a while, but when word got out about his true identity he was once more turned away from restaurants and snubbed in the street. James Whistler, with whom Oscar had once enjoyed a great if combative friendship, announced to a Paris restaurant, 'Wilde is working on *The Bugger's Opera*'. Oscar Browning failed to recognize him – or pretended not to. One of the few people to greet him warmly was the palmist Cheiro, whose prediction two years earlier had proved so horribly accurate. 'How good of you, my dear friend', said Oscar. 'Everyone cuts me now.'

Two final rays of light shone briefly into the panorama of gloom. *The Ballad of Reading Gaol* turned out to be a commercial success and, for the most part, a critical one too. He and Bosie patched over their mutual resentment and spent a few weeks wandering hand in hand around southern Italy; but even this pleasure was soon snuffed out. On the death of his brutish father, Bosie inherited the immense sum of £20,000. But he chose to give his former benefactor not a penny. 'I cannot afford to spend anything except on myself', he announced to a man now dying of poverty and sorrow. 'He has left me bleeding', wrote Oscar.

Oscar Wilde died on the afternoon of 30 November 1900, of cerebral meningitis. He was buried first in Bagneux, and his remains were moved in 1909 to Père Lachaise cemetery, where his tomb, designed by Jacob Epstein, can still be visited.

There are a thousand possible epitaphs for Oscar, most of them written by himself. But one way to remember him is to recall a story told by the comtesse Anna de Brémont, his mother's friend. It was a few months before Oscar's final sickness and death in Paris. The

countess was sitting in a café with friends and
he walked in. Afraid of what her companions
might say if they knew she and Oscar had
met before, she put up her fan and pretended
not to see him. Later one of her friends said
she would have liked to meet Oscar, if only
to 'find out what sort of monster he is'.

Ashamed of her cruel snub, the countess had
a sleepless night and went out early next
morning on a boat on the Seine. 'Good
morning, are you surprised to see me?
Surely not,' came a familiar voice. 'You
are not the only restless spirit in this great
Paris.' Oscar was in the mood to talk – about
the past. 'Life held to my lips a full-flavoured
cup, and I drank it to the dregs, the bitter and
the sweet. I found the sweet bitter and the
bitter sweet.'

She asked him why he no longer wrote, and
he answered, perhaps sadly, but more prob-

ably with the matter-of-fact tone that comes when even sadness is exhausted: 'Because I have written all there was to write. I wrote when I did not know life. Now that I know the meaning of life, I have no more to write.'

A winter scene

A truth ceases to be true when more than one person believes in it.
Phrases and Philosophies for the Use of the Young.

Modern morality consists in accepting the standard of one's age. I consider that for any man of culture to accept the standard of his age is a form of the grossest immorality.
The Picture of Dorian Gray.

W ickedness is a myth invented by good people to account for the curious attractiveness of others.

Phrases and Philosophies
for the Use of the Young.

The first duty in life is to be as artificial as possible. What the second duty is no one has yet discovered.

Phrases and Philosophies
for the Use of the Young.

If one tells the truth, one is sure, sooner or later, to be found out.

Phrases and Philosophies
for the Use of the Young.

M orality is simply the attitude we adopt to people whom we personally dis-like.

An Ideal Husband.

If you pretend to be good, the world takes you very seriously. If you pretend to be bad, it doesn't. Such is the astounding stupidity of optimism.

Lady Windermere's Fan.

M oderation is a fatal thing. Nothing succeeds like excess.

A Woman of No Importance.

If we lived long enough to see the results of our actions it may be that those who call themselves good would be sickened with a dull remorse, and those whom the world calls evil stirred by a noble joy.

The Critic as Artist.

LIFE AND TIMES

Julius Caesar
Hitler
Monet
Van Gogh
Beethoven
Mozart
Mother Teresa
Florence Nightingale
Anne Frank
Napoleon

LIFE AND TIMES

JFK
Martin Luther King
Marco Polo
Christopher Columbus
Stalin
William Shakespeare
Oscar Wilde
Castro
Gandhi
Einstein

FURTHER MINI SERIES
INCLUDE

ILLUSTRATED POETS

Robert Burns
Shakespeare
Oscar Wilde
Emily Dickinson
Christina Rossetti
Shakespeare's Love Sonnets

FURTHER MINI SERIES INCLUDE

HEROES OF THE WILD WEST

General Custer
Butch Cassidy and the Sundance Kid
Billy the Kid
Annie Oakley
Buffalo Bill
Geronimo
Wyatt Earp
Doc Holliday
Sitting Bull
Jesse James

FURTHER MINI SERIES INCLUDE

THEY DIED TOO YOUNG

Elvis
James Dean
Buddy Holly
Jimi Hendrix
Sid Vicious
Marc Bolan
Ayrton Senna
Marilyn Monroe
Jim Morrison

THEY DIED TOO YOUNG

Malcolm X
Kurt Cobain
River Phoenix
John Lennon
Glenn Miller
Isadora Duncan
Rudolph Valentino
Freddie Mercury
Bob Marley